THE LAND & THE SEA

THE LAND & THE SEA

Kyffin Williams

GOMER

First impression—1998
Second impression — 2001

ISBN 1 85902 553 6

This book is published with the support of the Arts Council of Wales.

Designed by Elgan Davies.
Printed in Wales at Gomer Press, Llandysul, Ceredigion.

For Rosalie

contents

AN INTUITIVE, AN OBSESSIVE, a driven character, a maverick poised between a deep melancholy and a warm and natural understanding of the absurd, Kyffin Williams is the central figure in contemporary Welsh painting. I say this not because of his achievements as a landscape and portrait painter, not because of his draughtsmanship and not because of his fluency as a writer, lecturer, cartoonist and raconteur. I say it because an image of Wales in the second half of the twentieth century is inconceivable without him. Kyffin has given form to the concept. He has recorded, through his oil paintings, his watercolours and his drawings, the spirit of a mountainous landscape and its people which we now use as our yardstick in visualising and understanding the Welshness of Wales.

Living close to the water's edge, looking across the Menai Strait from Anglesey to the mountains of Snowdonia, Kyffin has committed himself to making a record of his native land which extracts only its essential elements. The monumental, watchful nature of the mountains, the character of the hill farms and cottages, the dark clouds, the inhabitants of the land and the predatory nature of the Irish Sea—these are the inspiration for his work. But to all these elements the artist brings a strong and foreboding historical presence. His paintings are of a land at once both pre-Industrial Revolution and post-nuclear age. He knows instinctively that the power station at Wylfa Head, on the north coast of Anglesey, will be redundant long before the mountain cottages are abandoned and there is almost no reference in his work to those things which will disintegrate or become obsolete. He stands directly opposed to the American School of Photorealism, an art of extreme verisimilitude, where the registration plate of a Chevrolet will be reproduced with photographic accuracy. For a subject to command both his full attention and his devotion, Kyffin's instinct as an artist must be touched by its inherent sense of truth, its natural and historical place. It is the primeval rocks of Gwynedd and the heavy mists hanging over the Llanberis Pass, elements that had their place a thousand years ago as they will a thousand years from now, which inspire him. It is for this reason that sheep dogs in the mountains and children in the local school are as important to him as Snowdon itself.

In this, the first book to focus on the landscapes and seascapes, over sixty oil paintings, watercolours and drawings have been selected from public and private collections to show Kyffin's response to the interaction of the elements. Over a third of the works selected are of the sea, either breaking against the rocks at Trearddur or reflecting a fractured sun setting at Dinas Dinlle and it is here in these seascapes that we see Kyffin at the height of his achievements as a painter. His subject, hostile and fleeting under storm conditions, demands a degree of commitment, observation and understanding beyond the capacity of most contemporary painters and we must return to Emil Nolde, to Monet and before them to Courbet and Turner to find the rhythms, the turbulence and the emotive power of the sea expressed with such conviction.

It is in the late seascapes that Kyffin comes closer to pure, non-representational painting than at any other point in his work and he chooses the most violent conditions under which to work:

'October is the time for storms and it is then that I go to Trearddur to work among the rocks and bays, preferably when the storm is at its greatest and the noise of the turbulence most deafening. I have always remembered the noise and, in some ways, I have tried to interpret it in the vigour of the paint.'

He describes how from early childhood, he would watch the waves crashing over the reefs, during those October storms:

'We often rode on small ponies to see the damage done by the raging of the sea and to gaze on the wrecks that littered the coast. The lifeboat tradition of my family must have made me very conscious of the terrors of the storms.'

Understanding the cylindrical structure of the waves, watching the way that the cylinder is lost as the wave breaks and seeing the pattern repeated, so the artist makes detailed notes and drawings before returning to his studio to complete the painting, very often within a single day. His physical engagement with the canvas during the act of painting is both energetic and exhausting but one that springs from an intuitive and absolute commitment to his subject. 'All my past is in my painting,' he says, 'and not only my own past but the past of my ancestors too.' Using a palette knife to create a sense of movement within the paint which corresponds to the movement of the sea, the artist creates a tension between abstraction and topographical accuracy, the canvas becoming a means of linking the transient with the eternal. The viewer is drawn in by the tautness of the marks on the canvas as the original violence and power of the sea is re-created before them.

Kyffin Williams has often talked about his 'visual library', an unconscious image bank, developed over more than seventy years, in which he stores his knowledge of the land and the sea, of cloud formations and light and of weather conditions. From an early age, when out in the mountains, he began the process of 'seeing and retaining' so that information essential to the landscape painter became etched into his memory. But as a Welshman he is concerned not simply with the land as an isolated entity. He is concerned with the people and with their relationship to the land. The Welsh word *cynefin*, of which there is no direct equivalent in the English language, describes that relationship: the place of your birth and of your upbringing, the environment in which you live and to which you are naturally acclimatised. So at key points in this book we see the interaction between man and his environment. But the idea of a reclining or wandering figure, something which appears repeatedly in the British landscape tradition of the previous one hundred and fifty years, is alien to Kyffin. His figures stride, they confront, they are carried forward through blizzards and snowstorms, down the steep incline of a hillside and into wind and rain. They have purpose. They are rooted, and very often the character and momentum of the artist himself is echoed in his portrayal of these figures. In 'Farmer, Pont Llyfni', an isolated figure struggles against the elements under an immense blackened sky as six black crows fly towards a distant mountain range. In his first volume of autobiography, *Across the Straits*, Kyffin Williams talks of '. . . the mood that touches the seam of melancholy that is within most Welshmen, a melancholy that derives from the dark hills, the heavy clouds . . .' and nowhere is that mood more clearly illustrated than in this lyrical painting. The human drama, the sense of isolation and the solidity of the mountains are evoked with authority in each movement of the palette knife.

The Welsh landscape has been a valuable source of inspiration for British landscape painters for more than two hundred years and in the twentieth century some of our most prominent artists, John Piper, Graham Sutherland and David Bomberg amongst them, have produced outstanding work as a result of their contact with this landscape. But Kyffin Williams is the first native Welshman to take north Wales as his subject and to remain faithful to it throughout a long and prolific life. Where with Sutherland and Bomberg the concern is less with the actual landscape and more with the emotive landscape in the mind of the artist, in Kyffin Williams the two are both equally balanced and indivisible. The inner and the outer landscapes become inseparable. While he presents us at one level with a landscape exterior to himself he simultaneously communicates a landscape buried deep within his subconscious. The retentive, peripheral vision of a boy who spent his adolescence hunting in the mountains of Eryri became a focused, centred and passionate vision, a lifelong obsession. Paintings of great resonance and power have emerged, paintings which have the capacity to touch and to renew what is oldest in the human spirit at a time in our history when that spirit is undernourished and undervalued. It is these paintings which are the artist's gift both to Wales and to the British landscape tradition.

the LAND

I WAS LUCKY TO HAVE BEEN BORN in the lovely land of Gwynedd into a clerical family that had lived there for hundreds of years. We looked after the needs of generations of parishioners, lived comparatively easily and had time to absorb the beauty of that very special part of Britain. Some of my family farmed, introduced the swede and the iron plough to Anglesey and became wealthy from the copper mines to the north of the island.

Some painted the landscape around them and all of them must have absorbed the beauty of the land. I too inherited the love of the countryman for his native land, and subconsciously the landscape of Gwynedd and the mood of the land seeped into my youthful mind. Children never question why they like things because emotions come easily to them and at the age of five I must have been impressed by the lovely Ceiriog valley with its bluebells among the trees. At the age of seven in quarantine with chicken pox in a school dormitory in Anglesey, we were asked to write a poem about the snow outside. My poem was judged to be the best and I won a prize of sixpence. I have never forgotten that snow long ago, for the sky was of a deep ochre and umber and there was an immense silence.

Gwynedd was known to the Romans as Venedotia or the land of Venus for they too had fallen under its spell. In ancient times it stretched from Chester to Anglesey and as far south as the Dyfi valley. Today, its eastern border has retreated westward to the Conwy valley. It is a land of majestic mountains, rolling hills, of lovely fast-flowing rivers, and with a beautiful and varying coastline.

The whole of this land is dominated by the mighty shape of Snowdon or Yr Wyddfa in Welsh. In some strange way people relate themselves to it as it spreads its ridges in many directions. As far away as Aberdaron at the end of the Llŷn peninsula, Snowdon can be seen presiding over the landscape. It is a superb bit of geological architecture with its lakes and subsidiary peaks of Yr Aran, Y Lliwedd, Crib Goch and Crib y Ddysgl, and the whole of the county of Caernarfon pays court to it. Anglesey views it from across the Menai Strait but knows it is a land apart and remains secure in its insularity.

Meirionnydd is a different land; a place of lovely valleys, woods and streams; a more intimate land and one of greater charm than the county of Caernarfon. Cader Idris is a magnificent ridge without the imperious presence of Yr Wyddfa.

This is the land that has obsessed me throughout my life. My love of it is not superficial but deep, for my family have for so many generations had the same feelings for the land and its people. When I left art school I did not have to think what I should paint for my subject was deep inside me and waiting for me to record it.

On leaving the Ceiriog valley in Clwyd my family returned to Anglesey where I had been born. From a house above the Strait I could gaze at the mountains to the south little knowing that they were to become so very important to me. After two years in Anglesey we moved to south Caernarfonshire, to an ugly house near Cricieth and it was there that I became, for the first time, aware of the beauty of the land of Gwynedd. From the hill in front of our house I could see what appeared to me to be the whole of Wales. The Llŷn peninsula stretched away to the west, leaping away in a series of fascinating hills. Behind me the lovely yet unhappy Cwm Pennant nestling under the ponderous hump of Moel Hebog, the Tremadoc rocks, and behind them a distant view of Yr Arddu, Cnicht, the Moelwyn mountains, and even further away a glimpse of Arennig Fawr; then the whole exciting range of mountains that swung like the blade of a scythe towards the far away shape of St David's head and the Presely Hills. It is a staggering view and at the age of about fifteen it must have meant something to me. It may have lit a very slow fuse that later was to become a smouldering passion.

It was while I was living in south Caernarfonshire that I first began to follow the Ynysfor Foxhounds into the most remote valleys and over the highest mountains in Gwynedd. It was up among the rocks that I came across the hill farmers as they watched the hounds following the line of their enemy the fox. In cloud, in driving rain, and in the ochres of autumn, I watched these men and their dogs. I watched the clouds clearing the wet breasts of the hills and I saw the rock faces shining in the sun after a heavy shower. Once, I saw the brocken spectre on the slopes of Moel Ddu. A circular rainbow formed below the cliffs and at its base a huge figure of a man. I waved my stick and the gigantic figure waved his as well. Not many people have seen the brocken spectre. One morning, after a day of continual rain, I made my way to a meet of the hounds at Penygwryd. Under a clear blue sky the valley towards Beddgelert was invisible under what appeared to be a sea of milk, broken only by small rocky islands that emerged from the depths of Cwm Dyli. Away to the south-west the whiteness of the rising mist wandered to below Craig y Dinas and onwards to Beddgelert. Above the village rose Moel Hebog, clear and bright in the morning sun. As I watched, the cloud that clung to the valley below, began to break up. Wisps floated away to reveal the brackened hillsides and the farms far below me. It was all very improbable and unpaintable. On another day near Penygwryd I took my paints with me and was painting the cliffs of Y Lliwedd when the hounds moved away onto the rocky slopes of Glyder Fach. I stayed to paint and let them go without me. Painting was beginning to take precedence over the hunting. Even though hunting the fox in the mountains of Eryri had become part of my life, I have never painted the huntsmen and their hounds, but I have always remembered the farmers and their collies, and have put them down on my canvases for they are truly part of my landscape. The men could never have been able to work their hill farms without the help of their dogs and I have always been fascinated at their relationship.

Not only did I store up the visions of the landscape, the farmers and the sheepdogs in my mind but also the birds and the animals. I saw the buzzard and the peregrine, the ring ouzel and the dipper. Occasionally I saw a hen harrier as it quartered the moorlands, and the choughs as they whistled and wheeled around the cliffs of Snowdon. Apart from the thousands of foxes, I saw once, when high up on Moel Lefn, a mountain hare in its winter coat and, in the snow near Aberdunant, the footprints of the rare pine marten. All I saw was stored away in a library of memories that I refer to still when I am painting today.

I began to paint in all weathers for my hunting days in the mountains had made me impervious to the wind and the rain. I found that even if the rain filled my paintbox when falling on my palette it merely turned my paint into the heaviness of putty. I have always loved painting the snow and was able to stand gloveless before the easel when the temperature was below freezing point. As I began to work I felt the cold but after about a quarter of an hour the cold seemed to disappear and when, after about an hour and a half, my painting was finished, I found, invariably, that my hands were unusually warm. I suppose that total concentration created some sort of yoga.

For the first twenty-five years of my painting life I believed it to be necessary to paint in oils on the landscape but gradually I realised that an important element in any work is the interpretation. Working in the mountains and in the fields was useful because I gained a knowledge of the colour of Gwynedd but when this was stored in my mind I ceased to paint on the spot and worked entirely in my studio, creating works in oil that are painted from the very many pencil, ink and watercolour drawings that I make when out in the hills and valleys.

When I lived in south Caernarfonshire I found that the village of Llan Ffestiniog became my favourite place from which to paint the mountains and small farms. Away to the west, across the vale of Maentwrog, rose Moelwyn Mawr and Moelwyn Bach joined by the ragged ridge of Bwlch Stwlan. Sometimes they looked enormously high as they reared above the valley and when the snow covered them they could have been mistaken for the foot-hills of the Himalaya. When I was young and fit I used to dive down into the valley with my easel, paints and canvases, climb through the heavy bracken, before tackling the steep grass slopes above Llyn Stwlan. When the picture was finished I pegged the canvases together and holding them high above my head to prevent wayward bits of bracken making contact with the wet paint, I would return across the valley to where the village of Llan Ffestiniog spread itself like an Italian hill village. Often I walked across the valley to Tanygrisiau, a strangely attractive jumble of houses below gigantic slate tips. Quarrymen's cottages and terraces hid under rocky outcrops and streams tumbled down between them. The landscape was hard like the slate that came from it.

Beddgelert must be the most beautiful village in Wales, situated as it is where valleys and rivers come together below great mountains. I have stayed there many times in order to paint Yr Aran, Y Lliwedd and the exciting pass of Aberglaslyn. In the early years of the nineteenth century two well-known artists, Julius Caesar Ibbotson and John Warwick Smith were travelling nearby in a coach. Near the rocks of Carreg Bengam a storm burst over them, the lightning flashed and the terrified horses reared up between the shafts. Both artists were so impressed by the savagery of the occasion that they recorded it with two fine pictures.

Richard Wilson's great picture of Snowdon from Llyn Nantlle is one of the finest of a mountain that has ever been painted. Today one of the lakes has been drained away but the great ridge of Snowdon still fills the gap between Mynydd Mawr and Mynydd Drws-y-coed. I go there often and have done many paintings near the lake but, being a local man, I never feel that I can take the same liberties as did Wilson. Strangely, topographical accuracy is still important to me.

Everywhere in Gwynedd I see the stone farmhouses and cottages and the meandering stone walls that tie them all together into a fascinating unity. I have always loved to paint these buildings, maybe because of the people who lived in them or the abstract patterns they create. I am always conscious of the Welsh word *cynefin* which does not mean just landscape but a landscape with everything in it. The hardness of a scene appeals to me more than a softness and this may be because I prefer my work to be stark and possibly dramatic. There is certainly much hardness in Gwynedd and great contrasts of dark and light as when the sun bursts over a jagged ridge high up in the mountains. The impressionists would have found it difficult to paint my land.

In Gwynedd the seasons often appear to be exaggerated. In spring the east wind blows and the mountains retreat into a haze; but in the valleys the sycamore and willow burn like green and yellow candles against the still, cold winter hills. In summer the land attains a strange hibernation, for the mood is heavy and lacking in the stimulation that is necessary for an artist. The mountains become tame, the rivers flow slowly and the waterfalls cease to cascade, apart from in the month of August. There is an old Welsh saying, *Tri lli' Awst*, which means there are always three floods in August, and often they pour down the mountainsides to flood the summer-hard valleys. Autumn is the time of sea-mists that creep in from the south-west, dampening the old quarry villages above Caernarfon. October is the month of storms and it is then that I go to Trearddur, on the far west coast of Anglesey, to work among the rocks and the bays. In early November the land around Nanmor and Llanfrothen is at its most beautiful as the autumn colours coat the valleys and hills. There can be no more lovely area in the whole of Wales. The winter comes and then it is the most exciting time for the painter. Snowdon becomes blue-black and the bracken a brilliant red against it. It is at this time of year that Crib Goch lives up to the russet of its name. Winter is the time of dramatic contrasts that so stimulate me as a painter: the dark ridges against a wild white sky and the foaming waterfalls crashing over black rocks. This is the season I have dreamed about when, far from home, my thoughts have turned to the land that has made me a painter.

I have painted the mountains, the ridges, the screes and the green rain-soaked breasts of the hills. I have painted the lakes and the rivers, when they crash from rock to rock in exciting raging waterfalls. I have painted the castles, the farms, the cottages, the *corlannau* and the *beudai*, and of course the people. I have painted the Welsh Black cattle that make any field look even more green, and the beautiful Welsh mountain ponies that must be the most graceful animals in Britain. I have been lucky to have been born into such a land and I have been lucky to have been given a life that has been long enough for me to put down my appreciation of it.

PONIES, LLANFAIR-YNG-NGHORNWY

The parish is in the very north-west corner of Wales where, on a clear October day, I can see Ireland, the Isle of Man and the hills of Cumberland. This is where the ships from America or South Africa turn in order to make their run for Liverpool. This is a special place where, for two hundred years, my family have lived and loved the land.

It lies at the opposite end of the island from where I live but often I go there to watch the sun setting towards Ireland. One day I stopped on the narrow road above the sea and watched the sun shining on the sea as it stretched out towards the hills of Ireland. The silence was broken by a frenzied clatter of hooves as down the road galloped some magnificent Welsh mountain ponies, some chestnut, some black and some grey. The gate into the field in front of me was open and into it they charged, almost immediately to stop to crop the rich green grass that grew amidst the roughness of the sea-girt field.

I made a quick drawing of them but it was the mood that enabled me to paint the picture that eventually became part of an exhibition in the Royal Academy to celebrate the Silver Jubilee of Her Majesty the Queen.

Penrhiwiau

The long, low cottage above the Nantlle valley has always fascinated me; also the many cold and grey stone walls beside it that enclose the small green fields. It provided a scene that was so very paintable.

One day I knocked on the door of the cottage so that I could ask permission to draw in the fields. I heard a noise within and when the door opened I could see in the darkness the figure of Daniel Roberts, the old man who had lived there since he was a boy.

I asked him if I could go onto his land. There was a long pause broken by the single word, 'Why?'

'Because I would like to paint a picture of your cottage.'

'Why?'

'Because you have a lovely old cottage,' I replied.

He became almost talkative.

'What are you going to do with the picture?' he asked.

'Oh, someone might want to buy it,' I replied hopefully.

'Why?' he asked once again.

At this last question I felt that I was not getting very far, so thanking him for the permission he hadn't given I waved him goodbye and wandered away into his small and stony fields. Half an hour later the door of his cottage opened and he emerged with his dog. He walked towards me but did not stop to see what I was doing.

Across the valley below rises the high ground of Mynydd Mawr and behind it the hard microgranite intrusion of Yr Eifl. Beyond them the magical land of Llŷn with its hills, its valleys and its small fields stretches away to Aberdaron and the island of Bardsey.

I often wondered if old Daniel Roberts ever stopped to stare at the beauty of the view from Penrhiwiau.

Sunset over Llŷn

High above the Nantlle valley a straggle of houses wander above the slate tips. It took its name of Cesarea from its only chapel, but today the local council has seen fit to re-name it Y Fron. In these irreligious days the local geography has triumphed over the Bible. Local people must surely have felt some delight at adding to the confusion by placing incongruously in front of the chapel a bench bearing the heavily lettered name, Llandudno Junction.

Above Cesarea, between the quarry and Mynydd Mawr, is the small lake known as Llyn Ffynhonnau. In the last century it must have been used as a reservoir for the slate quarry in the valley, but today it is a reedy pool with the remnants of leats and banks that once combined a more sizeable area of water.

From the north side one can look across the water to where, in the distance, the humps of Y Gyrn Ddu and Y Gyrn Goch rise up with Yr Eifl and Tre'r Ceiri beyond. Further to the south-west the land of Llŷn, with its jumble of hills and valleys, stretches out to the south-west and the island of Bardsey.

I have done several paintings of Llyn Ffynhonnau and each time have exaggerated the size of the lake; but then it is the prerogative of the artist to do so if he wishes to create a special mood, and up there under the slopes of Mynydd Mawr there is a powerful mood.

As a young man Turner stood on the top of the mountain and drew the same view in his sketchbook. He was an artist who knew all about the importance of mood.

FARMER BELOW THE MOELWYN

Long ago, I remember an old colonel of the Gurkhas pointing across the Vale of Ffestiniog to where the snow-capped Moelwyn Mawr and Moelwyn Bach rose into the brilliant green-blue sky and telling me that the view was the nearest he had ever seen to his beloved Himalayas.

This painting was done from memory. I wanted to create that air of magic that often hangs over the Vale of Ffestiniog when the evening mists come down.

In 1755 Lord Lyttelton passed that way on his journey through Wales and the Vale of Ffestiniog. 'Not long ago,' he wrote, 'there died in that neighbourhood an honest Welsh farmer who was 105 years old. By his first wife he had 30 children, and 10 by his second wife, 4 by the third and 7 by two concubines. His youngest son was 84 years younger than his eldest brother and 800 persons descended from his body attended his funeral.' Truly, the Vale of Ffestiniog is a magical place.

WATERFALL, CWM GLAS

Kneeling beside the stream the water seems to fall out of the sky. It races from rock to rock, fanning over the larger ones or diving between the smaller as it flows headlong to join the river far below in Nant Peris.

I go up to the mountains after heavy rain, when they seem to have great reservoirs inside them from which the water bursts from every crack or gully. Streams that I have never seen before fall vertically over rock-faces, all appearing to be desperate to join the larger river in the valley. As each stream joins it, it swells and its roar becomes louder and more angry. The torrent that was born in every crevice above the valley grows wider, louder and more angry until it joins the sea.

I have looked at waterfalls all my life and the strength of their rocks and powers of their waters have reacted on me as wine might act on others. Waterfalls are nature at its most exciting and the excitement stimulates me to record them.

PENTREPELLA

Pentrepella crouches, a jumble of old stone houses, on the side of the mountain above the harbour of Holyhead. It used to look like an Italian hill village but now the council has decreed that the benefit of civilisation should be bestowed on the attractive group of houses. No longer do the inhabitants fill their buckets from a stand-pipe; electricity now lightens the houses—all with the result that immediately they become desirable residences and new people move in. However appropriate this might be, it has nevertheless made the appearance of the group of houses less attractive.

I painted this picture before too many alterations had taken place. The houses seemed to grow out of the mountainside and culminate with the solid shape of Tabor chapel. As I made my drawings for the picture, a Welsh mountain pony was playing a malicious game as it chased a small pig around a rough field. When the pig dived for refuge into a gorse bush the pony jumped into the middle of it driving out the squealing pig that immediately dived into another bush. This game went on and on until, worn out, the pig squeezed under a rough gate and escaped from its tormentor. Ponies have a strange antipathy towards pigs and this my reverend grandfather knew for he kept one in Gadlas, a cottage at the bottom of the hill below his rectory. Often the pony stopped outside the cottage and refused to go up the hill, but if he did, my grandfather would shout, 'Maggie Jones, send out the pig.' The door of the cottage would open to release a small pig that dashed up the hill to be followed furiously by an enraged pony.

I often make drawings of Pentrepella when I pass that way to draw the great cliffs that plunge into the sea near the South Stack.

AUTUMN ROAD, NANMOR

I believe that the land between Beddgelert and Penrhyndeudraeth could be the most beautiful in Wales. At its heart lies the lovely valley of Nanmor. From the wooded Hafod Llyn it wanders upward between the birches at Dolfriog and the tree-less rocks of Yr Arddu. The sun shines on Dolfriog and Moel Nanmor but the north side of Yr Arddu is cold and cheerless. Yet the valley always seems to be a happy place and I go there often in autumn to gaze at the bracken and the birch trees and to try to capture the glory of it all.

The valley is a great refuge for foxes and badgers and high up on the slopes of Moel Nanmor I have seen exotic llamas nibbling the short mountain grass. Buzzards mew above the trees and peregrines swoop from the black rocks of Yr Arddu.

At the top of the valley near the farm of Gelli-iago the view of the central mass of Eryri is breathtaking. It lies to the north so that the sun shines directly on to its jagged peaks, thereby making it difficult to paint, for no great shadows are created apart from Cwm Llan between Y Lliwedd and Yr Aran.

If this magnificent prospect is too great to be confined to a canvas, the beauty of the gentle valley of Nanmor forces me to paint it throughout the seasons, but it is in the autumn that I love it the most.

FARMER, PONT LLYFNI

Llyn Nantlle lies between the sharp ridges of Cwm Silyn and Drws-y-coed on one side and the roundness of Mynydd Mawr on the other, while behind it towards the east the precipices of Snowdon form a magnificent barrier, enclosing the valley and creating one of the grandest views in Wales.

It was this view that inspired Richard Wilson to create one of the finest paintings of a mountain in European Art. He painted two lakes whereas today there is only one, as the other was drained because of seepage into a nearby slate quarry.

Afon Llyfni flows from the lake and winds through the Nantlle valley towards Caernarfon Bay. At Pont Llyfni the whole magnificent view, enclosed by the lake, broadens into a panorama of hills, mountains, spurs and ridges, while always presiding in the distance is Snowdon itself.

One day, as I drove to Pwllheli in the snow, the clouds hung over the valley. Mynydd Mawr and Mynydd Drws-y-coed were faintly visible but Snowdon was hidden. A great weight of silence seemed to lie over the land. A farmer wandered along the road and the only noise came from the crows that were tearing at the body of a dead sheep. The mood was threatening, the farmer insignificant but the whole moved me to such an extent that, on my return to Anglesey, I painted what I believe to be one of my better landscapes.

WELSH BLACKS AT ABERFFRAW

A field will always be made to look richer if a herd of Welsh Blacks is grazing on it, for the darkness of their coats increase the intensity of the green; but when I painted this picture the sun was going down over the bay and the grass was turning to a more gentle russet.

Paintings of the Welsh landscape of the eighteenth and nineteenth centuries often show cattle in the fields or standing in a river, but these are invariably either red or roan in colour. I suppose they must have been shorthorn and possibly a few red Welsh Blacks. This may sound contradictory but the red genes were apt to be dominant until, by careful breeding, the blacks became more common until now in the twentieth century, it is rare for a Welsh Black cow to have a red calf.

Before the war, when I worked for some of the large estates on the Llŷn peninsula, I used to attend the sales of pedigree Welsh Blacks in Menai Bridge. One year an estate wanted a new bull, so one was bought and named Nanhoron Helmet. He was a magnificent animal but unfortunately his progeny tended to be red; so one tragic day the noble Nanhoron Helmet breathed his last in the Pwllheli slaughter house.

I have painted many pictures of Welsh Blacks but strangely they have never been successful when in a green field. This painting, I believe, is more successful than any of them.

SNOW, TŶ CWYFAN

At Porth Cwyfan, great reefs stretch from one headland to another causing the waves to crash upon them and in breaking their force, allow the nearby fields to remain safe from the fury of the storms. In one of these fields is the cottage farm of Tŷ Cwyfan.

It is an attractive shambles of cottage, boats, lobster pots, wooden shacks and innumerable posts which appear to remain vertical through the mutual security provided by rope and wire. Flocks of geese and guinea fowl wander among the old boats, a small dog barks a welcome for, as few people are to be seen, he always appears to be glad of the company of anyone who might be passing by.

If Tŷ Cwyfan is hidden by its screen of disorder, the ancient church of Llangwyfan stands resolute on the top of a grassy island contained by a high stone wall that is built upon the terrifying reefs. At high tide the church is surrounded by the sea and on days of storm the waves break over the old building that has withstood the elements since it was built in the fourteenth century. At one time the ringing of its bell might have warned sailors of the proximity of the reefs but today it is a curiosity that is accessible at low tide. Lovely flowers grow in the crevices of the rocks near the old church and oystercatchers fly and whistle above it.

Porth Cwyfan always draws me to it and I have done so much of my work along the coast. My great-grandfather rode along the cliffs nearby in 1854 and, seeing a ship about to break up on the rocks, managed to get a rope to its bowsprit, and saved the crew. I have always doubted if I would have the courage to follow his example.

TŶ CWYFAN

The fields of Tŷ Cwyfan reach the edge of the sea and some of the drawings I made of the small farm were from just above the shore. I painted this picture from one of them.

Using a considerable amount of artistic licence I tidied up the fields surrounding the buildings and simplified the untidy smallholding. Many artists would have welcomed the shambles but I found the jumble of boats, huts and lobster pots to be too confusing. Tŷ Cwyfan has for a long time been a reminder of the hundreds of similar cottage farms spread across Anglesey but soon it will be gone and a modern bungalow will take its place. I doubt if I will want to paint it.

Snow at Ogwen

The Ogwen valley was a lonely place in the eighteenth century when the road from London to Holyhead passed down the Conwy valley to the shore near Penmaen-mawr. From there the coaches crossed the Menai Strait at low tide and a boat ferried the passengers across a narrow stretch of water to a point where another coach carried them across Anglesey to Holyhead. The track through the dangerous mountains was used only by local people and farmers.

After the new road was made in the nineteenth century the wild and desolate Ogwen valley was visited by many more people who came to gaze at the magnificent peaks and also to climb them. Tryfan, three thousand feet of dark grey rock, dominates the whole area. From the valley three crests crown the top but from the north, on the side of the grassy Carneddau, the mountain rears skywards as a single spectacular peak in front of the forbidding mass of Glyder Fawr and Glyder Fach. Tryfan is the most magnificent single mountain in Wales.

Afon Llugwy and the headwaters of Afon Ogwen rise on the southern slopes of the Carneddau, the Llugwy to flow down to the Conwy valley and the sea and Afon Lloer and Afon Denau to pass in to Llyn Ogwen, shallow and grey, before Afon Ogwen bursts out, falling hundreds of feet, into Nant Ffrancon below.

The valley east of Llyn Ogwen is a brown and ochre valley of small farms but it is not a hospitable place and I am sure that many people making their way through it are glad when they have passed the lake and the great waterfall and have dived down into Nant Ffrancon and the more welcoming land beyond.

SEARCHING FOR SHEEP

I have painted many pictures of hill farmers in the snows of winter. It is then that they become heroes, wandering the frozen mountainsides with their dogs and searching for their sheep.

The fit sheep can stay alive for up to two weeks under the drifts that form against the stone walls that range over the hills or under the great boulders that cover the mountainsides of Gwynedd. Their breath creates some sort of an igloo and a small yellow hole in the snow can indicate to a farmer that the sheep are underneath it. The only sheep that are likely to die in the winter storms are the unhealthy ones.

Up on the mountain the farmer uses a long stick to prod through the snow and their dogs use their noses to search for the places where the sheep might be. Against the white of the snow the muted colours of the farmers's clothes gain their full value. The browns, the greys and the blacks become more intense than they are when contrasted against a green field. On a dark day in the winter the snow is never white but merely a very pale shade of grey that has subtle variations. The contrast with the dark rocks creates a visual excitement of which I never tire.

STORM OVER CRIB GOCH

Many years ago I was asked by the magistrates of Caernarfonshire to paint for them a full-length, life-size portrait of the much-respected Lord Morris of Borth-y-gest, a Lord of Appeal in Ordinary (a Law Lord). Lord Morris was a most genial man whose personality oozed goodwill and bonhomie: nevertheless, he had the reputation for handing out very heavy sentences.

When he stood before me to be painted the smiles disappeared and in their place I saw the face of the law at its most intimidating. It was this side of his personality that I painted so I was not surprised when the portrait was turned down by thirty-three votes to one.

I had been in Nant Peris when the clouds were down above Cwm Glas. A darkness covered the great cliffs and the land nearest to me was a mixture of umbers and ochres. I needed a large canvas quickly so I scraped down the noble Lord, sandpapered him, turned him horizontally and over his prostrate form I painted the rocks, the screes and the clouds of Nant Peris. Buried below the wilderness of the landscape I feel that Lord Morris of Borth-y-gest might have a smile on his face.

ICE ON LLYN IDWAL

Near the geological downfold below Clogwyn y Geifr and what is known as the Devil's Kitchen, Llyn Idwal has attracted many artists during the last two hundred and fifty years. It is not easy to paint for the subtleties of the rocks beyond demand the attention of the artist's eye and the further edge of the lake contrives to divide a picture into two areas of paint.

One day, I found that the lake had been frozen after days of heavy frost. The ice was strangely rippled as if a gentle wind had been blowing as the ice was being formed. Usually the water appears to be divorced from the land around but, when frozen, there appeared to be a unity that made the scene more attractive.

I drew the scene and as I did so, the wash of ink began to freeze creating a pleasant mottled texture on the paper. I have done many paintings and drawings when it has been freezing. Very often the pictures are failures but often the effect of the freezing process has improved what would otherwise have been a very dull drawing.

Autumn, Nanmor

I believe that the colours of autumn create greater problems for an artist than any other season of the year. And I believe that no great painting of it has ever been created. Constable never painted it and Turner only vaguely in his series at Petworth. Millais' blind girl has a brief splash of autumn in it, while the French impressionists, who worked so much in the open air, seldom risked painting it. The reason, I believe, lies in the fact that green and brown do not go well together and cancel each other out. That may be the reason why the impressionists only painted autumn trees beyond a river and not a field, and why the Group of Seven in Canada, when painting the fall, muted their greens to some sort of a greenish grey.

I love the autumn for its sense of melancholy seems to strike my need for sadness. A smile in a portrait is seldom successful whereas melancholy can be very moving. There is poetry in the dying of the year and mystery as well.

Nanmor is a lovely valley and is at its best in autumn. In this picture I have made my greens as yellow as possible so as not to clash with the bracken and to allow the cold stone walls to show their true colour.

Llŷn

The peninsula of Llŷn is a land apart. A very special and mysterious land of tumble-down hills and streams surrounded by a silver sea. Nothing is large in Llŷn for it is an intimate world of small roads, small fields and small villages.

Centuries ago the Irish from Leinster are supposed to have settled on the peninsula and the small, round stone huts to be found on the hills are known in Welsh as *cytiau'r Gwyddelod*, the Irishmen's dwellings. Indeed, the word 'Llŷn' is reputed to derive from Leinster.

The peninsula dives to the south-west towards Ireland and the Wicklow Mountains and from it I am always aware of the island across the sea.

This picture was painted from above the valley of Nant Gwrtheyrn, named after Vortigern the British king who, seeking sanctuary from his enemies, hid in this distant place. Inevitably, they found him and to escape, he hurled himself into the sea from a precipitous cliff named Carreg Llam, or Rock of the Jump, that is at the right-hand corner of this picture. Further westwards is the bay of Porth Dinllaen and the hills of Carn Fadrun and Mynydd Anelog.

Llŷn is the most lovely unspoilt land in Wales. I hope it remains so.

TEIFI POOLS

It was late March. The sky to the south-west was a bitter yellow and the clouds were of a mixture of ochre and warm grey. The wind was so icy that I could only make quick notes in my sketch book and hoped that my information would be enough for me to paint a picture of that fascinating place.

I believe the river Teifi to be the most beautiful in Wales; and we have lovely rivers in the north. Rising from the Teifi Pools it passes into the great Tregaron bog, one of the natural wonders of Wales. On it winds, fast flowing and full of salmon, past the little town of Llandysul, Cenarth where they fish from coracles, the castle of Cilgerran and then on to Cardigan and the open sea. It is a river of character.

The pools from which the Teifi flows nestle among brown-green hills above the village of Pontrhydfendigaid. No trees shelter them and the water is stained with acid rain. It is a lonely land that surrounds them and the track that wanders above them appears to lead to nowhere. It would be a melancholy place were it not for the view across Ceredigion, a pleasant land of small farms and people who, like the river Teifi, are of unusual character.

CARREG CENNEN

There are greater castles in Wales than Carreg Cennen. Some are more magnificent, some have been built more skilfully and have greater architectural merit, and some may have played a more important part in our historical past, but none of these can challenge the castle of Carreg Cennen in its claim to be the most romantic, mysterious and, maybe, forbidding of our mediaeval fortifications.

Macaulay, in his *Lays of Ancient Rome*, visualised an ancient building and described it 'as an eagle's nest hangs on the crest of purple Appenine'. So, too, does Carreg Cennen, but the hills are those more gentle ones of Carmarthenshire. The castle is certainly an eagle's nest as it crouches on a cliff high above the Cennen valley.

Carreg Cennen was a native Welsh castle but changed hands regularly over the war-torn centuries. Sometimes the English held it, sometimes the Welsh, but in 1462 orders were given for its destruction. Today it is a much-loved ruin.

I painted this oil from the south, above the Cennen valley and with the land stretching westward towards the blue hills of Pembrokeshire. There is a silence up there; Welsh mountain ponies wander among the rocks, crows and buzzards are in the sky and in the distance the unforgettable sight of Carreg Cennen.

COTTAGES, CESAREA

Stone walls, cottages, green fields and slate tips—these are what make up the strange broken land above Caernarfon. It is a hard land and at one time the dampness of it brought misery and tuberculosis to the people who lived there. Today the quarries are closed and only the aggressive tips remind us of the struggles of the last century.

The land around Rhosgadfan does not make me feel happy but I am so attracted by it that I return again and again to record an area that makes me believe that it died so many years ago.

The village of Cesarea sprawls above the Nantlle valley and boasts but one row of houses that could be called a terrace. In one of its houses lived Lizzie Jones, a poet whom I used to visit after drawing in the fields. She warmed me with cups of tea as we talked about her poetry. The last time I saw her before she died I asked her what she was writing and she told me that she was translating *The Screwtape Letters* into Welsh. It seemed to be very surreal.

One of the largest houses in Cesarea is known as Tŷ John Jones, Tal-sarn, for a powerful local preacher lived there. He may have been a powerful preacher but he is also famous for having been the progenitor of nearly all the worthy people of the vicinity.

One day, I was drawing on the road nearby when a little old lady came along with a sheep on the end of a short rope. I asked her the name of the sheep and she told me it was Elin.

'Oh,' I replied, 'is she Elin Jones?'

'No, no,' she said indignantly. 'No indeed, she is Elin Lloyd-Jones.'

COTTAGES, DEINIOLEN

I never feel that Deiniolen is a happy place, for the cottages are mean and huddle around the bowl of land that seems to empty towards the west to the town of Caernarfon. The lives of the people who lived there must have been hard for in the past tuberculosis must always have threatened them. The large church and the chapel do not appear to be part of the village and seem to have been placed there for respectability. Nevertheless, I go there often to prospect the area for subjects to paint. Maybe the melancholy of the place appeals to me, for seldom do I return home to Anglesey without some idea for a painting. Stone cottages are scattered under the hillsides surrounded by their few fields. There are stone walls, slate fencing posts and wire. There must be people there too, but seldom do I see them. I often wonder what they feel about their land or if they ever gaze out westwards when the sun is setting over Anglesey and beyond to the coast of Ireland. Somehow I do not associate Deiniolen with the sun.

It was October and the autumn sun shone from high above Snowdon and Crib Goch to light the leaves of the trees and to turn the pale green grass into a paler yellow. Capel Curig and the harder land of Snowdon is not far away, but here the land is more gentle and wooded as it falls away towards Betws-y-coed and the Conwy valley. At this spot the road eludes the heavy coating of coniferous trees and emerges into a different land of oaks and beech trees. This sudden glimpse of Snowdon and Crib Goch always seems to come as a surprise and, driving from England, I know that I am nearer home.

Snow above Deiniolen

The hard little village rests in a bowl under the mountain. At its lower end it opens up and far below one can see the Menai Strait, the flat land of Anglesey and Caernarfon Bay. Under the mountain a road leads diagonally across the hillside and, at the ridge at the top, Snowdon can be seen rising above the lake and town of Llanberis. At this spot I painted this picture with the old quarrymen's cottages nestling against the hill as if they were part of it.

This was a land of slate and the men who lived in the village and in the cottages scattered on the hillside all worked in the huge Dinorwic quarry. Some of them were part-time farmers who often enclosed their small fields with narrow bars of local slate. It is a damp land and the sea mists creep up from the distant sea enveloping the mean houses and bringing sadness to an area that once was riven by the curse of tuberculosis.

When the clouds clear, I go up to Deiniolen to draw the cottages and the winding roads. One day, I was drawing one of these small stone-built dwellings when a farmer came to watch what I was doing and he asked me if I wanted to buy it. I enquired how much he wanted for it.

'A hundred pounds,' he replied.

I didn't want his cottage but I asked what its name might be.

'Buarth y braich,' he replied. I asked him what it might mean. He spat and said, 'Well, I don't know what it means but I know for sure that Julius Caesar stabled his horses in it.'

SNOW IN NANT PERIS

The farm of Blaen Nant rests on a piece of grassy land under the towering cliffs of Nant Peris and close to where a stream flows from Cwm Glas in a series of waterfalls before it joins the river in the valley below.

Nobody lives there now but at shearing and dipping time there is much activity as the sheep are driven into the maze of small stone enclosures at the back of the farm. Huge rocks litter the fields and when the snow covers the land their darkness becomes even more intense. The feral goats, once so shy and inapproachable, now graze on the terraces above the precipitous cliffs across the narrow valley and sometimes raid the roadside litter bins.

From Blaen Nant one can see in the distance the solitary tower of Dolbadarn castle that has fascinated so many landscape painters. The greatest of these was Turner who was so inspired by its lonely presence amidst the towering mountains that he painted a picture that he was to deposit as his Diploma work on election to the Royal Academy.

Nant Peris is a lovely if frightening valley, narrower and more impressive than Glencoe, especially when seen from the bwlch at Pen-y-Pass from where the road seems to disappear into the depths of the valley below where Blaen Nant stands amongst its boulders and its rings of stone walls.

SUN AND SNOW, CRIB GOCH

Snow will always make the sky more obvious in a picture, for its own lack of colour will increase it in everything else. So the sky can become so many shades of grey, sometimes green, sometimes slate in colour but often a heavy shade of ochre. It was warm when I painted this picture, for the sun was trying to break through. I waited in the hope that it would, as I wanted it to shine on the snow below Crib Goch, but it never really did so and I had to be content with recording it as a faint presence in the sky, waiting to bathe the snow-bound valley in sunshine. I laid an undercoat of gold over the sky and then on top of it I painted a warm grey, allowing the undercoat to show through, as if the sun were about to come through the clouds and light up the whole valley.

FFRIDD LLWYN GORFAL

The old road to Cwm Bychan from Harlech climbs up from the town leaving the castle far below, a great stone shape above the sea and opposite the thin line of the hills of Llŷn. Close to Moel Goedog it turns and winding, climbing and dipping into hollows, it wanders towards the old farm of Gerddi Bluog. Before reaching it, it passes at a distance an isolated farm nestling under a hill with the sea beyond. This is Ffridd Llwyn Gorfal.

I do not know how it got its name, for there is no *ffridd* there today and no tree to soften the landscape. I believe that the house has been empty for many a year, for I have never seen a human being anywhere near it. It stands remote and with an element of sadness about it, for when the sun goes down behind it and above the sea, the shadows make it merge with the land around so that the old farm becomes almost invisible against the rocks and hills that surround it. I have passed that way for over fifty years and Ffridd Llwyn Gorfal has always stood empty yet resolute, maybe with memories within its walls of a time long ago when children laughed and played around it and the cows came in to be milked.

It is the sort of place around which the imagination can wander endlessly. I have painted so many pictures of it and, who knows, there may be many more.

SUN ABOVE GWYNANT

Looking westwards to the lake from above Cwm Dyli the sun often bursts through the cloud to shimmer on the water that seems to be held in the grasps of the nearby mountains. The contrast of the darkness of the land increases the brilliance of the light and it is this that forces me to paint it time and time again. Always I work from a new drawing, for the moments are never quite the same. The colour of the sun changes, as do the clouds and I record these differences on scraps of paper so that I can use this information in my studio.

It is the crack of dark against light that excites me, and that excitement inevitably increases the sensuality of the paint and the rhythm of the painting. Moel Hebog is the grey shape in the distance with its attendant hills of Moel yr Ogof and Moel Lefn.

SLATE TIP, CARMEL

High on the hillside above Caernarfon, huge mounds of slate rise up to dwarf the small cottages that crouch below them. Those who lived in them must have played their part in creating these monstrous intrusions onto a previously lovely landscape.

Maybe they got used to them, eventually looking upon them with affection. It was impossible to ignore them but I suppose that they had become part of their homeland.

I have drawn many of these slate tips in Bethesda, Llanberis and Blaenau Ffestiniog, but those near the villages of Rhosgadfan, Carmel and Cesarea are, to me, the most attractice—if attractive is an appropriate word to describe them. Maybe paintable is a better word, for it is the contrast between the bulk of the forbidding tip and the intimacy of the nearby cottages that intrigues the artist.

STREAM, PORTH CWYFAN

It is a slow moving stream that is usually filled with yellow irises. I did the drawing for this picture after they had been cleared, so that I was able to paint the light as it fell on the water. The little cottage of Tŷ Cwyfan is on the left and further away the church on its island, for at high tide the water surrounds it. I used a long canvas as I wanted a build-up of shapes culminating in the bell-tower in the centre. The composition is very simple, for seldom in my work do I complicate things by trying to lead the eye in and around the picture. I find that a flat design is usually more effective.

CARREG CENNEN

It was a raw day in early spring when I made this drawing from a hillside to the south of the castle. The light was not good and it might not have been a building at all for it looked more like a scab on a geological mound. The cold winter had sucked the colour from the land, and the distance faded away into an impenetrable grey. Nevertheless, a pale light broke through the clouds to touch the grassy slope below the castle, giving it a solidity that had not been there before.

Cwm Aelhir is a small valley above Llyn Peris at a point where the larger valley of Nant Peris begins to narrow. It is steep sided, covered in small trees and has its own herd of feral goats. They once mined copper in Cwm Aelhir but it could not have been a profitable undertaking for, even though there is red industrial spoil there, the shafts do not go deep.

I climbed up above Llyn Peris to draw Crib Goch in the distance, behind a large cliff. I climbed one of the huge stone walls on the mountainside and found below it the dead body of a fox. Bodies of animals and birds are seldom seen in the landscape for, in some mysterious way, they disappear in death. Only when man intervenes to cause a sudden death does the body of an animal or a bird lie where it fell or in a place to which it dragged itself. This fox must have been shot and wounded, and had lain under the shadow of the great wall. The disappearance of the bodies of animals, birds and fish is a mystery I will never solve.

EVENING SUN ON SNOWDON

As we look across to the mountains from Anglesey when the sun is going down on a summer evening, the Carneddau, Elidir Fawr, Crib Goch and Snowdon become tinged in a soft, warm glow, leaving the valley cold and blue-grey. Sometimes it is pink and sometimes a warm apricot colour. It is a time of day I love but I have seldom been able to paint it.

I wish sometimes that I could be a more gentle painter but I have learned from experience that my true self does not lie in such an interpretation of the world around me. At art school a student should learn what he can do and what he can't do. He must then develop what he can but must never be afraid of veering away occasionally from his usual work in order to explore the subtlety of things that do not come easily to him.

SUN OVER LLYN PADARN

As the sun rises over Snowdon and Crib Goch it bathes Nant Peris and Llyn Padarn in a pink and apricot glow. From Bryn'refail and Y Fach-wen it seems to hover over the high mountains and in a strange way diminishes them. Llanberis, lying in a lovely land, is not a lovely little town, but it is a solid and sensible one. I would not want to paint Llanberis, for what is to be recorded all around it is much more urgent and demanding.

From Bryn'refail the early sun makes Llanberis invisible, and in this watercolour it cannot be seen. This is one of the very few watercolours that I have worked on for more than an hour, for the sun posed problems and it took a time to resolve them.

TREFIGNATH CROMLECH

Anglesey is covered by many prehistoric burial places like the one at Trefignath. In some strange way we, the people of the island, relate to them as part of our own past. They were raised long before the Celts, the Romans, the Vikings or the Normans came to plunder and settle. Once covered, they now lie as tumbled memorials to someone who in his time was great.

They make intriguing shapes as their ancient stones seem to claw their way out of the ground and, in the effort, collapse in a jumble of rocks and stones. These cromlechs continually remind us of our past for they, along with *meini hirion*, or standing stones, can be seen in every parish on the island.

One day, I was painting two standing stones at Penrhos Feilw, near Holyhead, when the farmer came to see what I was doing. I asked him if he knew anything about the old stones and he said that he did. I pressed him to be a bit more specific and he took off his cap, scratched his head and informed me that they were very old. I told him that I was of the same opinion but that I would like to know how great was their antiquity.

He looked very serious, put his cap on and spat on the grass.

'Well,' he replied, 'I can tell you that they were here before I was born.'

These old stones seem to increase our insular security. They are so much a part of our island and, indeed, our heritage.

CLOUD ON SNOWDON

We, who live within sight of Snowdon, know the clouds that so often hide its upper ridges. They can hang heavily over them, dark grey-black shapes that can terrify those from the plains of England. They can play around the tops, dancing in and out of the cliffs and breasts of the grassy slopes, here one minute and gone the next; or they can sulk, a grey impenetrable mass eliminating every valley, cwm, *bwlch* or crag. On these days the waterfalls can be heard but not seen, for on such days the wind is seldom strong. When blowing a gale, the clouds race around the peak as if in a steeplechase on a very uneven course. They charge over a distant ridge and into a valley only to leap over a nearer one in a wild aerial scramble.

I have been brought up among the mountains or in sight of them and although I might not love the clouds I accept them as part of my own landscape and they form an important part of my artistic life.

SUN ABOVE CRIB GOCH

Crib Goch is one of my favourite mountains. I like the way it seems to crouch, I like the variety of its shapes while further up the valley at Pen-y-pass I love the way it seems to rear into the sky like a Himalayan peak.

In the evenings, when there is no cloud on the mountain, the setting sun will creep in between the top of Gyrn Las to turn the westward spur of Crib Goch into a pinnacle of gold. The valley at Gwastadnant stays cold and dark, while far up above it the sunlit mountain can be seen from the faraway flat lands of Anglesey.

Crib Goch is a fierce and crinkled ridge made up of a fine-grained volcanic lava which weathers to a rusty-brown colour that gives it its name of red ridge or crest. I especially love the jagged ridges and the thrusting peaks when there is a strong light behind them, for it is then that they emanate a power that is stimulating to me as a painter.

The feral goats graze high above the valley, moving cleverly among the precipitous terraces of rock. I have seen a stoat, superbly white in his ermine coat, darting amongst the rocks and once I came across a peregrine consuming a rock dove that it had smashed to the ground. I did not want it to fly away but when it did a pair of ravens appeared to finish the peregrine's meal.

My great uncle Andrew Ramsay, a former Director of the Geological Survey, did much geological work in Nant Peris and it is obvious, from his memoirs, that he had a great affection for the valley.

CAPEL TABOR, PENTREPELLA

I must have made hundreds of drawings of this group of cottages as they crouch below Holyhead Mountain. I have drawn them in ink, in pencil and in watercolour. I draw them because I like them. I like their shapes, I like their sturdy confidence and I like the way they seem to merge into the hill behind. I do not draw them specifically for a painting but because, I suppose, I have a constant desire to create. It is very satisfying to be able to record what I like. They may not be great works of art but they are important to me.

The drawing is done by cutting the wrong end of a brush into the shape of a wedge, and dipping it into the ink. The consequent line on the paper can then be either thick or thin and often produces a satisfying lost-and-found effect. I prefer to add all the watercolour when the ink is still wet, thereby uniting the drawing into a reasonable whole.

LLYN FFYNHONNAU

This is not really a lake but a small disused reservoir that served the needs of the slate quarries below. Nestling under the smooth shape of Mynydd Mawr it is now a reedy pool, a refuge for wild duck and snipe.

From the northern side I can look across it to where the Llŷn peninsula stretches away into the Irish Sea and even further to the Wicklow Mountains. Not many people pass this way for it is a melancholy place surrounded by rock, reed, bracken and heather.

Far below are the slate quarries, the village of Cesarea and the Nantlle valley that winds towards Snowdon under the cliffs of Craig Cwm Silyn and Mynydd Drws-y-coed.

I have done many paintings of this part of Gwynedd but never have achieved a masterpiece like the magnificent 'Snowdon from Llyn Nantlle' by Richard Wilson.

SNOWDON FROM LLYN LLAGI

This is a very large drawing and I did it in my studio from the rough notes I had made beside the lake. From it I painted a picture, trying to remember the colour. This drawing is merely tonal and because of that it is possible that it is more exciting than the oil, much as a black-and-white photograph seems to be more satisfactory than a coloured one.

The lake looks black below the cliffs on the north side of Y Cnicht. It lies high above the Nanmor valley and few people visit the lake apart from the farmers and the poachers who take the trout from it by using the illegal *styllen* or otter-board. Many years ago, when out hunting, I saw a fox jump from the great cliff above the lake, roll over on a bank below, and then run away in front of the hounds before escaping from them above Blaenau Ffestiniog.

Free from the shadow of the great cliff, the lake appears to shine as it stretches towards a narrow strip of yellow bank on the far side, so narrow it seems that were it to be breached the whole lake would drain into the valley hundreds of feet below. Away to the north-west the mountains of the Snowdon group range magnificently with Yr Aran to the west, then Snowdon and Y Lliwedd, and to the east the pink-brown shape of Crib Goch.

It is wise to choose a favourable day to reach Llyn Llagi for it lies far above the wooded valley amongst the wetlands of the higher ground. It is a long climb to the lake but a rewarding one. I always enjoy the remoteness of Llyn Llagi.

SUNSET, DYFFRYN CAMWY

To catch the full effect of a Patagonian sunset, it would be necessary to use a moving camera, for the winds are so strong that the sky, unable to stay still, appears to be agitated by a continual flicker of red and gold. I have never seen such beautiful sunsets as those that danced above the valley, forcing me to try to make some sense of them in watercolour. I failed many times but in this one I feel I may have come close to recording the excitement of it as the sun went down above the little village of Gaiman. The wind in Patagonia blows continually for the peninsula seems to be the meeting point of the weather that blasts from South Africa to the east and New Zealand to the west. The ferocious gusts exaggerate the danger for those who wish to climb the jagged peaks and the persistence of them lines the faces of the Welsh who live in this faraway land.

Gorsedd y Cwmwl (from Trevelin)

Gorsedd y Cwmwl, or throne in the clouds, rises high above Cwm Hyfryd, the Welsh valley in the Patagonian Andes. I made this drawing from the window of Tŷ Ni, the small house in which I was staying with the Señora Gwenonwy Berwyn de Jones, and Nita, Norma and Paulino, the Indians she was educating and who helped her in the house.

Tŷ Ni stood in a rough piece of ground in Trevelin, a village hidden in the trees near the banks of the Rio Percy. The mountains surround it, but dominating the landscape is Gorsedd y Cwmwl, a mountain battered by the Patagonian wind and snow-covered for most of the year. It rises to about nine thousand feet and is on the border that divides Argentina from Chile.

Winds from Gorsedd y Cwmwl roared with a noise like an express train from the sky around it, and used to crash with a terrifying noise against the window of my bedroom. It would have shattered it had the window not been hinged so that it merely bent and waited for the next blast to come.

This drawing was done in mid-summer but the snow was still lying low down on the mountain.

The little town of Esquel lies snugly in a valley surrounded by smooth red and green hills. It is very much a Spanish town, built to an insensitive grid pattern that appears to ignore the stream that meanders through it.

When I was staying there I used to climb up the hills to the west of the town, where Indians lived in shacks with their families and many scruffy mongrel dogs. Up there I often saw a neat little black bird with a rich chestnut back, but when I asked the local Welsh what might be its name, they said that they had never seen it. Finally, I consulted Ethel Morgan, a girl I had met in Wales the previous year.

'Oh,' she said knowledgeably, 'that is what we call a *robin goch*.' I had seen the *robin goch*, or red robin in Dyffryn Camwy and knew that it was a larger version of our robin at home. She consulted her sister and they discussed the matter in Spanish.

'My sister says it is a *pecco colorado*,' she informed me confidently; but I told her that I had been in Patagonia long enough to know that a *pecco colorado* was the Spanish for a *robin goch*.

Later I was to learn that more interested Welsh people called it a *siôl fach goch* or little red shawl, while ornithologists referred to it as a rufus-backed negrito.

the S E A

As I am an Anglesey man, the sea has been part of my life. My ancestors and relatives had been parsons, soldiers, sailors and lifeboatmen who had, from time to time, ventured into the storms that raged around the island to rescue those who were in danger of losing their lives when their ships had foundered.

So, naturally, I had been brought up on stories of bravery and tragedy, stories of my great-grandfather and grandfather leaving their island rectories to disappear into the wildness of the Irish Sea. Their reverend hands held the tiller and the crew believed themselves to be safe under the guidance of the established church. I was told how when the Cemlyn lifeboat returned from the fury of the sea, a man would be waiting with a hammer to break the ice that had bound the hands of the crew to their oars. I heard of the loss of the *Royal Charter*, bound for Liverpool from Australia. It had sheltered from south-west gales off the north coast of the island but the wind had veered north-west and hurled the boat onto the rocks at Moelfre. Australian gold-rush prospectors had to decide whether to jettison their wealth or keep it strapped to their waists. They chose the latter and perished.

With these stories of disaster filling my impressionable mind, it was the savagery of the sea around the island that remained predominantly with me. Waves breaking with a thunder and a crash. The flying spume whirling into the air, littering the fields above the shore. Years later, when living in London, I could cast my mind back to the island and the sound of those terrifying waves. When from my memory I used to paint the sea off Anglesey it invariably appeared white on my canvas, for the storms were more memorable than the days of calm.

The island of Anglesey is a comfortable size, yet from almost every parish it is possible to see the coast, even if the sea appears only as a golden sliver of light as the sun sets. The north coast is more wild and rocky but I prefer the south coast, for the sun shines on the sea as it wanders over the mountains of the mainland, touching the wave tops and creating paths of light towards the shore. I love to paint this light as much as I like to paint the waves of the north, but it is to the west of the island that the sea is most exciting. The reefs and cliffs from Rhoscolyn to South Stack have given me endless subjects, and I am often at Trearddur, watching and recording.

It was to a school at Trearddur that I was sent as a boarder at the age of six and it was there in a building above the sea that the atmosphere seeped in to me, perhaps all the more poignantly because of all the stories that I had heard as a very small boy. I began to understand the pattern of the sea throughout the seasons. As boys we swam every summer day off the rocks in the bay and once a master went fishing and returned with a pollock that, placed beside me, was longer, or taller, than my diminutive figure. In winter we got used to the storms and sometimes we rode along the cliffs on shaggy ponies to see the ships blown ashore in a gale of the night before. I can remember a Russian grain boat, *The Mary Moller*, fast on the rocks at Porth Dafarch and the captain, a tall man with a flowing beard, gazing phlegmatically from the cliffs at the wreck of his boat below him.

The cliffs at South Stack are the tallest on the island and when I was a boy I went there often to watch the multitude of sea birds as they crouched on the ledges or wheeled around in their hundreds above the waves. There were puffins, guillemots and razorbills, kittiwakes and black-backed gulls, and in the spring their cries echoed against the great Precambrian cliffs. From there I watched the Atlantic liners turning westward towards Ireland after passing close to the Skerries off Llanfair-yng-Nghornwy in the very furthest north-west corner of Wales. It was in this distant parish that my family became most closely associated with the sea.

In 1821 my great-grandparents, James and Frances Williams, were returning to their newly-built rectory when they saw a sailing packet, *The Alert*, strike a rock near the Skerries and sink almost immediately. There was no boat nearby to attempt a rescue. They were so horrified by this disaster that they decided to start a fund in order to buy what was probably the first lifeboat in Wales. While James raised funds, Frances painted a large picture of George IV landing at Holyhead in 1821. She made a very early lithograph of the painting from which she sold copies for seven shillings each. With the sale of these, and the efforts of her husband, a lifeboat was bought and stationed in the nearby bay of Cemlyn. The local farmers provided the oar-power and James became the coxwain.

The year of 1835 was a busy one for James. Not only did he go out in the Cemlyn lifeboat but he also saved the crew of the *Active* off Cemaes. As the boat was in danger of breaking up, he rode his horse into the sea where it swam near enough for him to throw a grapnel into the bowsprit shrowds. Later in the year he was riding near

Aberffraw when he saw the *Sarah* on the rocks near Trecastell. He immediately got a line aboard and saved the crew. I don't know if Frances was there to witness this rescue but she painted a lovely picture of it that is now in Oriel Ynys Môn, Llangefni. For these two rescues James was awarded the Albert Medal, later changed to the gold medal of the Royal National Lifeboat Institution. My great-grandmother supported her husband in all his efforts in saving lives and during a severe storm, when a northerly gale prevented the Holyhead lifeboat from reaching a sick lighthouse man on the Skerries rock, she went out with her medicine chest in the Cemlyn boat and gave him the help he needed. In 1854, when James was sixty-two years of age, the iron-screw steamer *Olinda* struck some rocks near the Harry Furlong reefs. This time his place at the tiller was taken by my grandfather.

My grandfather, who was born in the rectory in Llanfair-yng-Nghornwy became rector of the parish of Boduan in Llŷn and from there he became the coxwain of both the Porth Dinllaen lifeboat on the north of the peninsula and of the Aber-soch boat on the southern side. When he first came to Boduan in 1862 a great storm drove fourteen boats ashore at Porth Dinllaen and the local people merely watched as, one by one, the crew were washed from the rigging into the Irish Sea. My grandfather managed to stimulate the bystanders into action and with their help managed to save the lives of twenty-four sailors.

With the Aber-soch lifeboat he rescued the crew of the *Kenilworth* that was breaking up on Sarn Badrig, St Patrick's Causeway, the bouldery bar off Llanbedr, near Harlech. When he rescued the crew of the *Dusty Miller* the captain gave him the ship's bell that I remember ringing when I was a small boy. When my grandfather returned to Anglesey to minister to the parishioners of Llanrhuddlad it was decided to move the Cemlyn boat to the more populated Cemaes that was further away from the dreaded Harry Furlongs. This so infuriated my grandfather that he went up to London to object. The angry octogenarian, armed with a marline spike, struck such terror into the minds of the officials of the RNLI that they relented. The boat stayed at Cemlyn but was moved the week after my grandfather died at the age of ninety. He had received the silver medal of the RNLI and the bronze, together with a second service clasp.

There have been many lifeboat heroes in Anglesey since the first boat was placed at Cemlyn in 1828. On the centenary of that occasion, celebrations were held in Llanfair-yng-Nghornwy. An eager young man from the BBC came to interview me. Placing me against a boat in front of my house he began to question me:

'Tell me, Mr Williams, what did it feel like to go out in a lifeboat in a storm a hundred and fifty years ago?'

More recently Coxwain Richard Evans of the Moelfre boat was awarded two gold medals by the RNLI. In 1959 he rescued the crew of the *Hindlea*, a coaster that struck the rocks at the same place as the *Royal Charter* had been lost a hundred years before. During the rescue his lifeboat was washed by a huge wave onto the deck of the *Hindlea* only to be washed off again by another. For this rescue Richard Evans was awarded his first gold medal and seven years later he received another after saving the crew of the Greek motor vessel, the *Nafsiporos*.

One of the most remarkable wrecks on the coast of Anglesey took place in the early years of the eighteenth century. A smuggler from Llanfair-yng-Nghornwy went out in heavy seas to meet a boat from the Isle of Man bringing an illicit cargo of gin. A gale blew up and in the raging seas he failed to meet the boat but found two small boys huddled together on a raft. He rescued them and found homes for them in the farms of Mynachdy and Maes. They were about six years old and could speak no language known to the inhabitants of the parish. One day, Mr Thomas of Maes found his small lodger putting a splint on the broken leg of a chicken. The leg mended and soon he became famous as a bone-setter; his descendants become well-known throughout Britain for their knowledge of orthopaedics. We were told that he probably came from Spain but it remains a fascinating mystery.

I suppose that, with a family background associated so strongly with the sea, it would have been strange had I not been drawn to paint the storms as well as the calms around Anglesey. I know the landscape so well that I can decide with ease what part of the island to go to in order to paint the weather to the greatest advantage. I love the shore at Llanddwyn when the sun is over Yr Eifl in distant Llŷn, and Aberffraw with its Penrhyn farms high above Caernarfon Bay. There are fine reefs at Porth Cwyfan and along the coast the waves, in a south-west gale, seem to be as big as houses. At South Stack I have spent many days gazing out to sea, drawing, painting and absorbing the immensity of it all as the sea-birds wailed and choughs flew among the rocks and the heather. To the north in the parishes of Llanrhuddlad and Llanfair-yng-Nghornwy I feel at home because of the history of my family in that land. Often I go there to watch the sun going down over the hills of Ireland. The sun burns deep red and suddenly, as it dips over the horizon, I see an emerald flash and it has gone. I love the sunsets over the sea. The sun is golden above the cloud bank but when it glows behind it, it becomes a lovely shade of coral and the lower it sinks the paler its pathway across the sea. I also love the sea mists as, silently, they creep in from the south-west smothering the land in a cloak of mystery. Most of all I love the sea when the wind blows into a storm and the waves crash onto the rocks in a ferocity of noise and power. I try to interpret the power by the handling of the paint but to communicate the terrifying noise is more difficult and I find that the only way to do so is to make great contrasts of dark and light. I find that this satisfies and also stimulates me.

The Menai Strait, that broke through at the same time as the inland sea near Holyhead was formed, is a wandering stretch of water that must be almost unique in Britain. From north-east to south-west it stretches from Penmon to Caernarfon Bay, from the broad Lafan Sands to Abermenai where it joins, once again, the Irish Sea. The tides race backwards and forwards, flowing one way on the Caernarfon side and another nearer to the island. Some of the woods that edge the water grow as they did when the Romans crossed the Strait. The rocks between Beaumaris and Menai Bridge are Precambrian in age but elsewhere are younger shales, marls and limestones.

It is at Pwllfanogl on the island shore that I live alongside a small harbour. It is a sheltered spot tucked away under the trees and safe from the full fury of the western gales. I have yet to see a wave breaking in the harbour. It is ideally suited for the life of a painter of the land and the sea for I can decide, on looking across to the mountains beyond the Strait, if it would be better to paint the land or the sea, the mountains or the island.

Only once has the sea invaded my house. It crept in silently through the front door, through the back door and up through the drains in the middle of the house. Even though there had been a high tide, together with two weeks of gales in the Atlantic, I was unprepared. Philosophically I sat on the stairs while my carpets floated around below me. At the turn of the tide the sea left as silently as it had come.

I believe that in painting the sea an artist paints his own personality more deeply than in any other kind of painting, for the picture becomes almost abstract; the moving sea allowing no firm objects to distract and the paint itself becomes the extension of the artist's emotions. I can get so immersed in the sea on my canvas that I find I am almost part of it. I don't know if the pictures are any the better for it but I do believe my seascapes to be among my best works.

It is possible that the influence of those stories I had been told as a child have helped to make me a painter of the sea. In the history of art I have been moved by the calm of the seascapes of Van de Velde and Brooking, by the storms of Turner and Courbet but above all, it has been the abiding influence of the sea itself, always there and always changing. All through my life I have looked at the sea, storing up a great knowledge of it. I know how the sun rests on it, I know how the waves break onto the shore or over the reefs and I know its many colours. This knowledge has given to me a natural love that luckily turned into what is so important to any artist: an obsession.

STORM OVER CAERNARFON BAY

At the height of the battle between land and sea, the storms seem to hurl themselves against the rocky coast. Squalls and waves break over the cliffs and rocks; shafts of light from behind the dark clouds shine on the wetness of the land. This is one of the skirmishes that have continued since our geological world began and the battle will not cease for as long a time as has already been. I am fascinated by the blankets of rain that sweep across the sea during a storm or in the many showers that blow in from the south-west. Sometimes the sun is hidden behind them and when they have passed it bursts suddenly over the sea before being extinguished once again by yet another blanket of rain.

SUNSET, DINAS DINLLE

The sunset moves me more deeply than sunrise. Maybe I am a pessimist and the end of the day has a deeper mood than the dawn. It is possible that the fact that the sun sets over the sea in my part of the world, gives it a greater feeling of emptiness and a greater melancholy. Whatever the reasons, I can look at the sun for an hour as slowly it descends from the duck-egg blue down through the golden-tipped cloud bank to where it hangs briefly, a deep coral shade in the midst of the burnished sky around it.

At Christmas time I often go to Dinas Dinlle where the sun sets toward Ireland and the Wicklow Mountains. From the site of an old British fort a shingle bank stretches towards another fortification that was built to deter the improbable arrival of Napoleon Bonaparte. Much further to the south in 1797 his troops made a very half-hearted invasion at Fishguard. Drunk and without any provisions they were soon made captives and the sun set on the last invasion of Britain.

The Wave, Trearddur

When I was a boy I used to dive on these rocks when the weather was fine, for the school where I lived for six years was close to the shore. I loved the storms and when they were at their most furious we used to walk along the shore and the cliffs and wonder at the power of the waters and the breaking waves. They excited me in those faraway days and they do so now when I am seventy years older. I still wander along the shore: the noise of the storm is the same and the waves that break over the rocks hurl themselves into the air with the same ferocity that I remember from so long ago.

It was only in the nineteenth century that artists became fascinated by the single wave. It was the time of the Romantic movement that stressed the possibility of disaster, the wildness of nature and man's apprehension of what was to come. The breaking wave had not previously been considered as a subject for an artist but its masculine vigour and threat of tragedy appealed to artists at that particular time. Even if his waves were not entirely convincing, I have always loved the way that they were painted by Gustave Courbet for he was able to create the mood of a storm. Emil Nolde, a man who had intimate knowledge of the sea, painted convincing waves a hundred years later and Joan Eardley, in the middle of the 20th century, carried on the tradition of painting the wild sea and its crashing waves when she worked in the open air with the storms wailing around her near the little Scottish village of Catterline.

Sunset, Fedw Fawr

On the left of the picture are the quarries from which the limestone blocks were taken to build some of the great castles of Gwynedd and the majestic bridges that join Anglesey to the mainland: but they are not features of great beauty and look at their best as dark shapes against the setting sun. So I paint them like that and concentrate on the beauty of the sky and the sea and the subtlety of the swiftly-changing light as the sun dips behind the cloudbank.

I have painted this scene so many times and every time I witness it there is a slight difference that makes every visit a new and worthwhile experience.

Sun over the bay, Llanddwyn

Across Caernarfon Bay the hills of Llŷn stretch southward to Uwchmynydd opposite the holy island of Bardsey. From Llanddwyn they are dominated by the three summits of Yr Eifl that plunges into the sea at Carreg Llam, a cliff from which Vortigern is said to have leaped in order to escape from his enemies. It is a lovely line of hills and I can watch it for hours as it changes in the sun or as the clouds form to the west. It seems as if the hills attract the weather when the wind is from the south-west and the clouds collect over them before moving north-east up the Nantlle valley to Snowdon.

The island of Llanddwyn, a Precambrian jumble of rocks, juts out towards Llŷn. It is said that Saint Dwynwen, a girl who had been crossed in love, retreated there and lived to console others who had suffered in a similar way, but Llanddwyn now is a happy place and the island is a sanctuary for rare birds and wildflowers.

I have done many paintings of Llanddwyn and hundreds of drawings have filled my sketchbooks. I have no doubt that I will be walking along the sands of Llanddwyn Bay for many years to come and gazing across to the fascinating hills of Llŷn.

Light over the sea, Llanddwyn

One of the joys of the great sweep of the shore at Llanddwyn is the view of the hills of the Llŷn peninsula as, getting smaller and more distant, they seem to finger their way westward before disappearing at the island of Bardsey, Ynys Enlli. I love those varying shapes, some pointed, some rounded and love their changing colours.

The water between Llanddwyn and Llŷn is known as Caernarfon Bay and the light on it changes continually.

At the time I painted this picture it was pearly, for the sun was trying to break through a thin veil of cloud and its brightness was spent on the sandy shore.

WAVE, PORTH CWYFAN

Waves during a storm can be terrifying for they become living things; violent and angry, they rage and roar and attack the land. After they have broken, the undertow hisses with frustration before rousing itself once more for another assault.

I like to go down to Porth Cwyfan when there is a storm in Caernarfon Bay. The waves seem to rear as high as houses before they break and give a strange stimulus to my nervous system.

I love the noise, the energy and the whiteness of the waves. They make my mind and body tingle. That is the time when I know that I must dash home and put it all down before the mood has blown away.

Coast, Porth Dafarch

It is a wild and jagged coast between the Trearddur and Holyhead. Near Porth Dafarch and South Stack the cliffs rise and split, creating reefs and islands, while out at sea the turbulent waters create one of the most dangerous races along the whole of the Welsh coast.

Crows nest in the cliffs as do peregrines, while on the cliffs of South Stack the real seabirds gather on the narrow ledges.

It is possible that I exaggerate the contrast of light and dark in my paintings of the sea but it is a way of interpreting the battle that wages continually between the power of the water and the obduracy of the land.

Evening, Morfa Conwy

As the sun goes down over the Menai Strait it appears to bathe the Anglesey shore with a gentle, pink light. Its reflection makes a path across the broader waters but disappears as it reaches the mud flats of Morfa Conwy.

There is a legend that beneath the shallow waters lies an ancient palace known as Llys Helyg. Large stones can be seen at a very low tide but the story must have something to do with the Celtic imagination.

To the left of this picture the great rock of Penmaen-mawr looms above the sea. It was there, in prehistoric times, that a factory flourished and produced hand axes of such quality that they were highly prized in Europe. In our time the 'granite' quarry has continued to employ local people.

ROUGH SEA, RHOSNEIGR

Often a painting of the sea demands a long canvas for the immensity of it seems to stretch the eye as waves break on the shore. I like painting on a long canvas, for the dragging of the brush or knife along it is physically and sensuously satisfying. I can whip out the spray from the top of a wave more easily or control that ill-defined area where the sky and the horizon merge in a tantalising problem of comprehension.

There are only three colours in this picture. The restricted use of black, white and yellow ochre can accentuate the drama in a seascape.

STORM, PORTH CWYFAN

The storm from the south-west was raging beyond the black rocks while I stood on a sheltered shore clutching a small sketchpad and trying to prevent the wind from tearing it from my grasp. I tried to record in a few frenzied lines the wildness and the ferocity of the white water. All I was able to do was to put down in a personal short-hand enough information so that, back in my studio, I could interpret the marks on the paper and create from them a true image of the storm.

The best way to paint the drama of such a scene is to restrict the colour range. Too many colours distract from a simple message and in this picture I used only ivory black, flake white and yellow ochre.

SUNSET, PENMON

So often the beauty of a sunset is increased by the pattern of the clouds that appear to be molten in the western sky. Such a view often becomes too complicated for an artist, and even if he is brave enough to embark on such a project he risks creating a work that comes dangerously close to vulgarity. The sunset is certainly a challenge.

When I go to Penmon on an evening in June I hope that the higher clouds have blown away and that the golden ball of the sun hovers momentarily over a cloud bank, for I know that before it disappears, it will create a line of gold. There are times when the sun bursts through the cloud bank, not in its molten brilliance but in a more muted coral.

This painting is an attempt to interpret that glorious coral in a simple, uncluttered sky.

LIVERPOOL BAY

Throughout the year the sea to the north of the island does not invite me to paint it. It is a cruel sea and for centuries it has hurled ships onto the rocky coast of north Anglesey, breaking them up and drowning many who sailed in them. Nevertheless, I do paint the waters of Liverpool Bay and the work I produce verges on the abstract, for in that way I feel more free to interpret the mood of the sea that stretches northward towards the Isle of Man.

I know where to go in order to see rare seabirds along that northern coast. At Cemlyn I watch the terns, at Fedw Fawr the rare black guillemots, and off Penmon I have watched gannets plunging into the choppy sea.

Storm, Trearddur

When the wind is blowing a gale force I leave my home on the Menai Strait and make my way across the island to Trearddur where I know the storm will be crashing against the rocks and over the many reefs that lie around that rugged coast.

These great storms have always excited me and I seem to be stimulated by the noise and energy of the waves – to such an extent that, when I transfer my frenzied scribbles onto canvas, my own energy attacks the canvas in an attempt to interpret the primeval force of the sea.

These paintings are not easy to control for often they try to take over and I lose my tones in a confusion of white wave and spray. In some ways I feel that the painting of a storm at sea is like the riding of a high-spirited horse that seems determined to bolt. Part of the excitement lies in the possibility of disaster.

The painting of a rough sea enables an artist to indulge in the sensuousness of pigment, the fluid richness of the oil medium. Such pictures are difficult to paint in watercolour and impossible in tempera.

Autumn Storm, Trearddur

One day, as the storm blew in from the west, I visited an old friend whose house was only a stone's throw from where the waves were breaking. Further out in the bay the storm crashed against the reefs hurling the spray into the air and driving it in balls of spume over the rocks and shore.

I stood in a room overlooking the sea and saw through the salt-sprayed windows the turbulence in the bay. I am easily exhilarated by the ferocity of the sea, so I had to ask for a piece of paper so that I could make notes in lines and in words for a picture that was forming in my mind. What I jotted would probably have been unintelligible to anyone else but it was enough for me to paint this picture.

It is important, but not essential, for a marine painter to have a deep knowledge of the sea. Certainly van de Velde, van de Capelle and Emil Nolde were brought up near the coast, but Turner, Courbet and Joan Eardley were not; their work benefits from the excitement of discovery and not so much from knowledge.

I have lived for most of my life near the sea. If I am not looking at it, I am visualising it. Waves break in my mind and the sun shines on the water. Sometimes I believe I can hear the noise of the storms and the lapping of the gentle waves as they break on a summer shore.

WAVES BREAKING OVER REEF, TREARDDUR

I have spent hours watching the waves as they race across the sea: rearing high into the air like a wild animal, they fall, spent and impotent, to be drawn back to the waters from which they come.

I love the spray as it is whipped off wave crests by the wind. I love the cylindrical cavern beneath the breaking wave and I love the lace of the foam as it darts here and there before retreating into the undertow.

My personal chemistry demands the excitement of a storm at sea, so it is only natural that I should paint, again and again, this particular expression of the ferocity of nature that has continued since the beginning of time.

SUNSET OVER POINT LYNAS

Many people might not think that I had painted this picture for it is rather pale and there are no hard outlines that are sometimes considered to be my signature. Maybe it could have been a little darker but my main consideration was to make the coral sun shine through the clouds with a true brilliance. Unusually, I achieved this quite early in my painting and, knowing how easy it is to lose the freshness and shine of the sun, I felt it wiser to leave well alone. It may be unusual but, nevertheless, I feel I did achieve something in the painting of it.

Point Lynas, the most northernly point in Wales, is where the Liverpool pilots used to join the great liners on their way to Liverpool.

STORM, TREARDDUR

I have always wanted to convey the noise of a storm as well as the wild and visual aspect. It may be that this is not possible but I believe that by making very strong contrasts in tone some sort of cacophony can be created. Consequently, I try to force the contrasts in this exercise in make-believe. But, of course, it may be an outpouring of my natural neurosis, for I believe that highly-strung artists do tend to jump their tones. I must have used acres of paper in my attempts to catch the wildness of the sea. I have drawn in ink and in watercolour but usually I prefer to use the pencil for, in doing so, I am more able to control my work in a high wind. Sometimes, as in this watercolour, I am able to achieve what I had intended by other means.

EVENING ON THE MENAI

The Menai Strait meanders from the shallow waters between Conwy and Ynys Seiriol to join the Irish Sea once more at Caernarfon Bay. The shores of Gwynedd and Anglesey are gentle and wooded, so that the strait has a calm beauty that contrasts with the distant mountains to the south.

The Romans under Suetonius Paulinus and Agricola had to cross the strait in order to conquer the island. The Vikings from Dublin sailed their longboats into these sheltered waters and in the year 1100 the Normans, under Hugh Lupus, Earl of Chester, celebrated their success with a drunken roistering at about the spot where I painted this picture. At the height of their celebration, King Magnus of Norway anchored his longboat offshore in order to find out the meaning of the unseemly noise. Hugh Lupus, angered at the sight of the Viking ships, rode his horse out into the shallow water brandishing his sword and swearing at those who appeared to be interfering with his festivities. King Magnus, standing in the prow of his ship, drew his bow and shot dead the intemperate Earl. As far as I can find out, the Vikings never returned and the Normans, demoralised by the death of their leader, felt it wiser to stay away from the island for a considerable time.

Many years ago, I lived quite close to where I painted this watercolour. I know it all so well and I love the mystery of the scene as the sun sets over the coast.

SUNSET, MOEL Y DON

The Romans crossed the strait at Moel y Don and they may have witnessed a scene not very different from the one I saw when painting this watercolour. They would have marched north-westwards to their fort at Holyhead, some of them from Italy and some of them mercenaries from different parts of the Roman Empire. They may have crossed to Ireland, but Anglesey was really the western limit of their empire.

There are many houses and towns clustered along the banks of the Menai Strait today, but at sunset they merge into the darkness of the land and the golden sun creates a scene that has remained the same over thousands of years.

THE GIUDECCA

The island lies to the south of the city of Venice and beyond the broad waterway through which liners and merchant ships pass. These ships appear to be enormous as they dwarf the ancient buildings on either side. From a wooden landing stage on the Zattere on the main island the Giudecca makes a fascinating shape against the sun, with the two churches of the Redentore and Le Zitelle on the main waterway and with the well-known shape of San Giorgio Maggiore dominating the eastern end, opposite St Mark's Cathedral.

It is advisable to rise early in the morning if an artist wishes to paint in Venice, for later in the day the visitors and the small boys of Venice vie with each other as they crowd around an artist, offering criticism or advice.

From Zattere the sun rises above San Giorgio and marks its path across the waterway before breaking in golden waves against the barges and landing stages.

Venice is an enchanted city that everyone should visit. I have been there many times and the memories are of what must be the most beautiful city in the world, a city-state that nurtured great artists who have meant so much to me. Giorgione and Titian were artistic giants but it is the vigorous painting of Tintoretto that appeals to me the most. The excitement of his brushstrokes creates an artistic electricity that somehow gets through to my own nervous chemistry.

GRAND CANAL, VENICE

I wanted to capture the shimmers of light as it reflected off the water. It is a strange little drawing but in some ways achieves what I had intended. I have never been able to see strong colour in Venice: instead I see the pearly light that Francesco Guardi reproduced so brilliantly in his small paintings. The diffused light created by the sea acts as a sieve that softens the strength of any powerful colour and, in doing so, gives to Venice its unique attraction.

VENICE FROM THE GARDENS

A visit to Venice has always been to me a pilgrimage to pay homage to its passionate and sensuous art. Florence was cooler and more classical and Siena more refined and inhibited, but Venice with its merchants and its wealth gave rise to a more exotic school of painting from which so much of the romantic art of Europe had its origins.

If its art is sumptuous, it only reflects the beauty of this strange and fascinating city with its canals, churches and palazzos. In the fourteenth, fifteenth and sixteenth centuries it must have been the most colourful city in Europe, with the ships of a great navy at anchor, their vivid sails blowing in the wind. Today, the liners that sail between the main island and the Giudecca create another, yet different, fascination.

The excitement of Venice lies in its difference and one of the greatest differences is the light. This is not a rich colour, for the light reflecting off the water creates a subtlety that has attracted a great many artists who have travelled far to record it over the last two hundred and forty years.

This picture is an attempt to capture that light and in some ways I think I succeeded, but after I had finished it I realised I had made the library near the campanile one floor too high. This annoyed me but had I tried to alter it I felt the picture would have suffered.

ACKNOWLEDGEMENTS AND DETAILS OF WORKS

I am greatly indebted to Nicholas Sinclair for the sensitivity, dedication and professionalism that he has shown in the preparation of this book. I am most grateful to him for the excellence of his photography and for his thoughtful preface. His help and encouragement have been invaluable. This book is dedicated to his mother.

I would also like to show my gratitude to Mairwen Prys Jones for her patience in preparing this book, to Elgan Davies for his skill in designing it and to Dr Margaret Wood for explaining to me the complexities of the geological structure of my native land.

Finally, I would like to acknowledge the encouragement shown to me for fifty years by the National Library of Wales, an institution that has done so much for art in Wales.

I am grateful also to those institutions and private collectors who own the paintings reproduced in this book for permission to photograph the work and reproduce it here.

page

18/19	Ponies, Llanfair-yng Nghornwy, 1974, 36 x 48
20/21	Penrhiwiau, 1992, 30 x 30
22/23	Sunset over Llŷn, 1990, 30 x 30
24/25	Farmer Below The Moelwyn, 1982, 36 x 48
26/27	Waterfall, Cwm Glas, 1988, HTV, 48 x 48
28/29	Pentrepella, 1972, 36 x 54
30/31	Autumn Road, Nanmor, 1997, 20 x 24
32/33	Farmer, Pontllyfni, 1971, 30 x 50
34/35	Welsh Blacks at Aberffraw, 1985, 20 x 30
36/37	Snow, Tŷ Cwyfan, 1997, 30 x 50
38/39	Tŷ Cwyfan, 1997, 20 x 30
40/41	Snow at Ogwen, 1972, 30 x 50
42/43	Searching for Sheep, 1996, 32 x 54
44/45	Storm over Crib Goch, 1973, 32 x 54

46/47	Ice on Llyn Idwal, 1991, 30 x 30
48/49	Autumn, Nanmor 1996, 24 x 24
50/51	Llŷn, 1985, 22 x 40
52/53	Teifi Pools, 1990, 36 x 36
54/55	Carreg Cennen, 1989, National Library of Wales 30 x 30
56/57	Cottages, Cesarea 1987, National Library of Wales 20 x 36
58/59	Cottages, Deiniolen, 1986, 20 x 24
60/61	Snowdon from the East, 1997, 24 x 24
62/63	Snow above Deiniolen, 1987, 30 x 50
64/65	Snow in Nant Peris, 1982, 48 x 48
66/67	Sun and Snow, Crib Goch, 1994, 20 x 24
68/69	Ffridd Llwyn Gorfal, 1996, 30 x 50
70/71	Sun above Gwynant, 1997, 24 x 24

SUNSET, PENMON